HIT OR MYTH

For my mother, who faced reality too many times—thanks.

And for Janelle Cooper—the wind beneath Jeff's wings.

Revised
and
Updated

HIT OR MYTH

An Analysis of Target Systems for Practical Training in Defensive Shooting

Louis Awerbuck

PALADIN PRESS • BOULDER, COLORADO

Also by Louis Awerbuck:

Combat Shotgun (video)
More Tactical Reality
Only Hits Count (video)
Safe at Home (video)
Tactical Reality

Hit or Myth, Revised and Updated:
An Analysis of Target Systems for Practical Training in Defensive Shooting
by Louis Awerbuck

Copyright © 2007 by Louis Awerbuck

ISBN 10: 1-58160-605-2
ISBN 13: 978-1-58160-605-8
Printed in the United States of America

Published by Paladin Press, a division of
Paladin Enterprises, Inc.
Gunbarrel Tech Center
7077 Winchester Circle
Boulder, Colorado 80301 USA
+1.303.443.7250

Direct inquiries and/or orders to the above address.

Visit our Web site at www.paladin-press.com

TABLE OF CONTENTS

WARNING

Firearms are potentially dangerous and must be handled responsibly by individual trainees and experienced shooters alike. The technical information presented here on firearms handling, training, and shooting inevitably reflects the author's beliefs and experience with particular firearms and training techniques under specific circumstances that the reader cannot duplicate exactly. Therefore, the information in this book is presented *for academic study only* and should be approached with great caution. This book is not intended to serve as a replacement for professional instruction under a qualified instructor.

INTRODUCTION

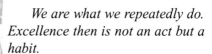

We are what we repeatedly do.
Excellence then is not an act but a
habit.

—Aristotle

We're not losing because the bad guys are better trained.
We're losing because we're beating ourselves.

Maybe the bad guy is faster or more accurate, or has more
plain dumb luck, but that's maybe 5 percent of the time. There's
nothing you can do about that, but there is a lot you can do with
your training regimen to improve the other 95 percent.

On a regular basis in deadly-force encounters, adept shooters
are missing their mark. While this is widely attributed to panic and
a lack of front sight focus (looking at the target instead of having
your focal plane on the front sight while firing), there are other
vitally important aspects to be taken into consideration.

The object of this book is to present some ideas to improve
current range training thinking. It is not another "instant expert"
autobiography. Obviously there is something vastly lacking with
current theories—if this book helps just one Good Guy make it by
picking up one small hint from the following logic, its objective
will have been realized.

CHAPTER 1

BOOT CAMP

Remember when you trained by the book in boot camp? Everything seemed perfectly logical the way it was explained. You followed the rules, and the training drills were executed with clockwork precision.

Then came the dark clouds of war. You rode off into the setting sun to do your bit—and two minutes after you arrived on the battlefield you found the instructors had lied to you. The only way to get the job done was to throw away the book and start all over.

The underlying fallacy of your prior training was that the enemy and the battlefield had absolutely *no correlation* to the range training you'd undergone. It just wasn't what they said it would be.

Similarly, many of the modern small-arms training techniques bear no relation to the realities of a street confrontation. To all intents and purposes the mechanical manipulations of the shooter stay the same, but the *target* and *surroundings* totally change the tactical problem. "Tactical" under these circumstances includes the manner in which you deliver the projectile(s), both from a timing and a directional point of view.

"Generic" option targets (humanoid in shape, with a squared-off head and torso) set up for El Presidente range drill (three targets 1 meter apart, 10 yards distant from shootist).

To illustrate this line of thinking and, indeed, as an abstract example of the logic behind this book, let's use the El Presidente range drill as an oft-quoted measure of a shooter's ability to handle a street scenario. El Presidente begins with the holstered trainee facing 180° away from evenly spaced targets—at a distance of 10 meters. On the "go" signal, the shooter executes a 180° pivot, fires two rounds to the body of each of the three targets, reloads, and fires an additional two rounds into the body of each of the three targets.

The score is "Comstocked," i.e., the overall time is divided into the score and a factor is obtained. A polished performer can consistently execute the drill in 7–8 seconds with a "near-perfect" score.

There's just one little snag here. First, apart from the fact that we've just gone back to the boot camp syndrome, were the hits in the paper targets *really* good street hits? The answer, to be brutally honest, is—probably not.

Graphic targets set up for El Presidente. Different elevations and angles, even though they are one-dimensional paper, force the shootist to have to think and identify. (The trainee will benefit most if he isn't shown the target scenario before commencement of the exercise.)

Before we move on to analyzing the whys and wherefores, let's extend the range drill one step further to a Demi-Presidente. This is the same as the Presidente, but instead of torso hits after the reload, the trainee is required to fire one head shot at each of the three targets. "Expected" overall time for the drill is the same as the Presidente. Note the word "expected" is in quotes—this is explained in Chapter 2.

And last in the Presidential race is the Tactical Presidente: one round in each of two torsos, two rounds in the third, reload, and one round to the head of each of the first two targets fired upon.

Reholster and turn to Chapter 2 . . .

CHAPTER 2

THE TIME-LIMIT THEORY

An honest analysis of Chapter 1 brings some interesting facts to light, the first of which is the "expected" overall time completion for a range drill. This is all very well and good, as long as the shooter understands it's a *range drill* and does very little toward simulating taking on three adversaries in the street.

There is no such thing as a static time limit to win an armed confrontation, basically because of one conveniently forgotten aspect. Range targets, save for the more exotic systems, *don't simulate reality*. For the most part the vital zones are too big and forgiving, the targets usually face straight on at belt-buckle to belt-buckle elevation, or the direct opposite—a moving target smoothly tracking sideways at 40 miles per hour (mph).

If the instructor doesn't simulate a street target or scenario, what *fighting* benefit does the trainee get? Let's be honest—zero.

So bang goes the time-limit theory. The only time limit you have is to put in accurate, damaging fire before it is done unto you.

Backing up to the initial Presidente: the 8-second "high-scoring" shooter has demonstrated excellent accuracy and gun handling but has done very little toward improving his multiple-assailant fighting ability. The reasons for this are many and varied. First, who can seriously believe that one man with a handgun can put four accurate rounds into the vital zones of each of three attacking assailants (including a reload) in *8 seconds*?! And starting off at 30 feet no less? If all three were standing, unmoving, and facing straight on, why didn't you just assassinate them via one shot in the head and be done with it?

The underlying basis of the training is supposed to be defending yourself from an assailant or assailants, with a view to stopping their actions before they put you into your grave.

An attacker on the move can cover approximately 20 feet in just over a second—so there goes your time limit "reality," plus 20 of the 30-odd feet got swallowed up in 1 second. Now we have three of these cretins, bobbing and weaving, at different heights and different angles. Is the Presidente all of a sudden starting to look a little shaky as a representative street training drill?

Moving right along to the Demi-Presidente . . .

If you can't virtually guarantee the easier (and quicker) body hits *for real*, how are you *for real* going to make the head shots in a Demi-Presidente? You aren't.

The Tactical Presidente is a much more rational tactical approach to the problem. But, again, for real, every time in the street it'll be different, and it would be foolhardy to *always* practice the drill in the same firing sequence.

What this all boils down to is to take the "accepted" range training drills for what they are and don't assume that they reflect street reality.

Let it also clearly be stated, at this stage of proceedings, that the Presidente exercises were designed by Jeff Cooper to get a "read" on an individual's mechanical pistol accuracy and manipulation capabilities. They were *not* designed as a training drill, even though they were based on an actual incident.

The Time-limit Theory

What follows in Chapter 3 is an in-depth look at what is probably the biggest and least analyzed problem of them all—target realism and vital hit zone definition when you're under pressure.

CHAPTER 3

TARGETS

This is not a training manual. It is an attempted insight into the ever-present problems of defensive shooting, studied from an uncommon perspective.

Granted, there are certain "givens"—panic, fear, tunnel vision under stress, loss of sight focus, trigger control—all covered in the past ad nauseam. Unfortunately, much as they've been analyzed and developed, the basic problem still remains: adept range performers are losing in the street.

With a view to the premise that maybe nobody is looking at what is possibly the biggest cause of street failure, we go on to—targets.

For the purposes of this text, we are going on the assumption that our "patient" is a competent marksman and is adept in the fields of gun handling and tactics. He can control his emotions, but still had a problem resolving an armed encounter in the street.

Inflate three party balloons to approximately 6 inches in diameter and another three to approximately 3 inches in diameter. Suspend the three larger balloons at about 4 feet 6 inches from the ground, 4

While a finite shot is available on the erratically moving rear target (black hat), it must be surgically placed to ensure the immediate incapacitation of the "hostile" and the safety of the two "innocents" in the foreground. A lot different than three static, one-dimensional cardboard targets . . .

feet apart. Then suspend the other balloons each 18 inches directly above the three big balloons, all hanging from thin thread.

Wait for a 5-mph wind, step back 30 feet—and go ahead with a Demi-Presidente drill. Not as easy as on paper targets!

Now set it up again, but this time the three large balloons are set at 4 feet, 4 feet 6 inches, and 5 feet, respectively. Two of the targets should be 3 feet apart, and the third is 5 feet from one of the others. The three smaller balloons are similarly suspended above the "torsos," but this time not directly above the larger targets. Wait for the wind and shoot the drill again.

Getting more difficult? Sure it is. Taking longer to get the hits? Sure you are. Nobody said anything about Life being fair. The sad part is that at this stage we've only *started* approaching a street-realistic Demi-Presidente target simulation.

Run the drill again, this time firing the first rounds at the center target, which is now at 20 feet, with the other two remaining at 30.

This is the difference between *beginning* to set up street realism and merely firing a mechanical range drill . . . and so far you've had relatively easy for-real torso hit areas, believe it or not.

Scenario: You're in a semidark alley, confronted by—you guessed it!—three armed thugs, approximately 10 meters distant. On uneven ground, with difficult-to-discern vital zones, you have no choice but to defend yourself with a handgun. How's that 8-second Presidente looking now?

We're going to leave the target problem for a while to discuss some other potential problems, but we will return to it later. Let it also be said that this is not a long-winded diatribe aimed at the Presidente or its variations. The drill has merely been used as an abstract example to illustrate a point of view.

CHAPTER 4

SEQUENCE OF FIRE

It's interesting to compare the 19th-century shooter with the 21st-century misser.

A hundred years ago our forebears had "inaccurate" weaponry and very little ammunition—and hit what they were shooting at. Today, for the most part, we have precision equipment and oodles of ammo—and miss the mark more often than not.

Coincidentally, the 19th-century adage was "Beware of the one-gun man." A hundred years later it's "Spray and pray." One can only gather from this that, as with many other things, we've lost the ability to do it *right*.

John Steinbeck's observation that "the final weapon is the brain; all else is supplemental" surely fits defensive shooting to a T. While the "Well, I've got more in the magazine if I miss the target the first 10 times" syndrome is a big contributor to the spray-and-pray brigade, it is not solely to blame.

If you blaze away at an assailant like there's no tomorrow, there probably won't be a tomorrow. But what of the man who does everything "right" and still doesn't hit his mark? Maybe his

range training was based on *inadequate target simulation* and *set-in-stone firing sequences.*
Does the term "boot camp" ring a bell?
Selective memory pervades many training ranges today. It is too often conveniently forgotten that the shooter is morally, legally, and ethically responsible for the *terminal* resting place of every projectile he launches downrange.

In essence, this complicates matters in the street, while—save for normal range safety considerations—it doesn't enter into the picture when "paper-punching" on the range.

For real, you not only have to impact the adversary in a vital zone and stop his deadly-force action, you must also ensure that you *do not miss.* If you miss, not only do you still have the immediate problem of self-protection, you also have the secondary problem of a projectile that you instigated winging its way toward the schoolyard.

It's all very well telling a trainee, "You have one in the "B" zone—probably good enough."
It isn't good enough!

It wasn't good enough shooting the balloons in Chapter 3—and it definitely isn't going to be good enough in the street. So what we did is to delude the shooter into thinking he's fighting at street level, when all he's really doing is practicing paper-punching accuracy. (Colonel Cooper's definition of "marksmanship" is hitting a living, breathing target *on demand,* right now, starting from cold.)

A terrific training aid, but one that can be very misleading if not used correctly, is the knock-down steel target. More on this later, but it is often, through misuse, the classic example of the preceding paragraphs.

Let's take one more ride to the shooting range and work on some commonly accepted rules:

1. With a handgun, always fire twice at the torso.
Ballistically, this is probably a great idea—in theory, it

The sequence and rate of fire are dictated by which of the five targets are dedicated as the hostile(s). (In this scenario, the rear three targets are set into erratic motion, all independent of each other. Innocent bystanders are not expendable!)

increases the probability of an assailant's ceasing his attack. Another oft-cited reason is to make sure you get "at least one good hit."

But if you got only one good hit, where did the second bullet *terminate*? Or does selective amnesia apply only on the practice range and "don't call me" when it goes down for real?

Firing continuous rounds individually as needed is easier and gives more consistent hits on a *moving, attacking* human target. You can excel at firing twice as a matter of course into a *nonmoving,* facing-on paper target, but training to *always* do this in the street is looking for trouble. Unless you are very, very close, it probably isn't going to work. The extension of this is the hammer (first round sighted, second unsighted and fired immediately after the first). Here, as with everything else, the objective is to make absolutely sure of your sight picture on a moving target. With the hammer executed mechanically correct, if the sight picture was bad, *both* shots are off the mark.

So what is the answer? The answer is to deliver accurate fire to a vital zone in *whatever sequence it takes* to cause your attacker to cease hostilities—and every encounter will be different.

2. **If you hit him twice in the chest area with a handgun and he doesn't go down, it's pointless firing at the body again.**

Well, for real, what are you going to do? The Automatic Failure Drill (two to the body, one to the head) is great, as long as the head presents itself as a target. For real, often the body is all you have to shoot at, or vice versa, for that matter. You may *have* to shoot 10 rounds at the body because *tactically* you are forced to.

Bottom line? Don't go on the assumption that the street hoodlum will present himself to you as the paper target on the regimented range. Do some serious thinking in your training regimen to vary target scenarios to *realistically* simulate street conditions.

Brew some coffee, take a seat, and have a look at Chapter 5. It gets worse . . .

CHAPTER 5

ANGLES AND MOVEMENT

So far we've touched on the basics, again bearing in mind that the trainee "patient" is proficient in the field of sight picture, trigger control, firing grip, etc., and is an accomplished marksman.

Well, you say, what can get worse that what we've already covered?

Basically, two things: angles and movement.

First, playing the angles. Step back 7 feet from a "generic" option-type target and then step 10 feet to your right. Fire several rounds at the target, which is usually 18–20 inches in width. Inspect your hits. In the center of the X-ring where you wanted them, right?

Wrong!

Simulating street reality, the hits should have been on the extreme edge of the X-ring on the side of the target nearest your shooting position.

Why? Because if the target were human and three-dimensional, and you take the angle of fire into consideration, hits in the center of the X-ring would have entered the assailant's right breast—not an immediately incapacitating wound. Similarly, hits on the far side of the X-ring would have left the bad guy totally unscathed.

This begins to illustrate a huge problem—training on one-dimensional targets for a three-dimensional confrontation.

Here is where it gets confusing! If you were shooting on an option target marked with A, B, and C zones, a hit in the B zone on the near side of the target is better than one in either the A or C zone, fired from the specific angle and distance regulated at the beginning of this chapter.

We've already established that a center A zone hit would have entered and exited the simulated human attacker's right breast. A bullet hole in the C zone merely indicates a flesh wound across the back. Impacting the B zone gives a diagonal bullet entry in line with his vitals.

So, yes, while face-on—as in Chapter 4—only dead-center hits count, we now have a situation where off-center hits on a one-dimensional target are tactically better than those impacting the center!

Here comes the rub.

A. It is extremely difficult to visualize a one-dimensional target in three-dimensional terms, which is *essential* for serious defensive training.
B. Instructors insist on hits "in the center."

Center hits on an *angled one-dimensional* range target *do not* correspond to vital zone hits on a similarly angled three-dimensional target. It's against the laws of geometry.

Hits in the center of the X-ring should be required *only* when the trainee is deemed to be practicing a direct face-on confrontation. For street simulation, the angle of incidence and corresponding off-center hits must be taken into consideration—and practiced.

Angles, angles, angles! If only one of these two targets is designated hostile—bearing in mind that both targets are bobbing, weaving, and moving laterally left and right, independent of each other—Colonel Cooper's Rule 4 ("Be sure of your target") becomes sacrosanct. Be sure of your target and its surroundings.

Similarly, elevation has to be taken into consideration. Taking journalistic license, let's assume you have dropped to a quick kneeling position—perhaps to angle a head shot upward to protect bystanders from a horizontally overpenetrating bullet.

If your "normal" standing position point of aim is in line with the eye sockets, you will now need to hold lower. If you don't, the bullet path will run from above the eye sockets through the top of the skull—probably not an immediately traumatic blow.

This becomes even more of a problem at close distances with high sight-line weapons, such as the M4 rifle, where one normally has to hold high because of the marked difference between bore line and sight line.

Hopefully, thus far you have been given some food for

thought. The following chapters will continue to "play the angles" and discuss motion—both yours and the target's.

CHAPTER 6

REALISTICALLY SIMULATING MOTION

Quotation heard in Utah in the late 1800s: "Forgive me, Friend, for I am about to shoot where thou art standing."

Looking past the wry humor, one can gain valuable insight into why so many firefight rounds go astray. If you turn the quotation 180° and put the "target" in line with the shooter and then move the target as the shooter *decides* to fire, the result is obvious. The projectile impacts where the assailant *was* positioned—but no longer *is* at the moment of hammer sear release.

Average response time is two-fifths to three-fifths of a second. Remember the gentleman who covered 20 feet in just over a second in Chapter 2? If you don't "track" him with the sights and at the same time *press* the trigger, you will not even have the satisfaction of a mediocre hit. If he runs east to west across your path, and you fire two-fifths to three-fifths of a second after he started running—without moving the firearm from its original point of aim—you will miss your target by approximately 8 *feet!* (This from an initial sight picture at only 7 yards.)

It's worth thinking about. In fact, it's terrifying. Granted, encounters are usually closer than 7 yards, but often they are not.

If the shooter were farther away, the "miss" would be even greater, all other factors being equal. Obviously, if he were closer, you would miss by less. Some consolation!

Taking one step deeper into the analysis mire: If your straight-on attacker is exhibiting the typical "weaving" motion as he approaches at speed, what will happen if you don't "track" the vital hit zone—firing three-fifths of a second after you get your sight picture? If he weaves to his right, you will shoot to his left. Similarly, if he moves left, you will shoot to his right.

Now picture the attack. He's alternating left and right on approach—and you're impacting right and left of the aiming point you had each time before you dumped on the trigger three-fifths of a second later.

Bingo!

Easy-to-hit laterally moving option target.

Laterally moving, spring-mounted, swiveling three-dimensional target.

All of a sudden our ace "combat" shooter is shooting anywhere from a 2-foot to a 4-foot group at 5 yards, because the target *isn't what it was on the training drills*. (Incidentally, this is the man who can fire two rounds into a paper X-ring in 2 seconds, from 10 yards—and has assumed that the street is that simple.)

Here's where it all goes to poo-poo.

The Monday-morning quarterback says, "He didn't focus on his front sight." Well, in this case our "patient" *did*. What he *didn't* do was track his target, putting on gradual trigger pressure.

The quarterback says, "Always fire twice at the torso." Well, if he were shooting a 2-foot group with individual rounds, what is he relying on now—a "lucky" hit? We are responsible for *all* the projectiles we fire—and their *terminal* resting place.

The QB says, "The hits must go in quickly." Well, sure, they must, or you're buzzard meat. But they *must impact a vital zone.*

Adding a "hostage" who moves independently of the "bad guy" cranks up the complexity factor.

If you don't hit what you're shooting at, the whole objective goes by the board. Remember, we're talking of self-defense with small arms, not a cover-fire, full-scale military operation.

If you have the luxury of a head shot, can it be *guaranteed* on a weaving target at 5 yards as quickly as three head shots on three nonmoving option targets at double the distance? Think about it.

You can't give "expected" times for specific distances. For real, you have to impact your selected target as fast as you can and *still guarantee the hit*—terrain, target movement, threat level, etc., will, for the most part, dictate your tactical delivery of projectiles.

There's more . . .

If we're all agreed so far, the next natural progression is to have the availability of a moving target for our training—to simulate *human* movement.

The easiest way to go is to erect a laterally moving driven system, but there are three flaws:

1. It's expensive.
2. It moves on too smooth a path, allowing the trainee to "lead" the target and get lucky hits—and it is not representative of characteristic human physical motion.
3. Unless a huge arc of fire is available on the shooting range, frontal and diagonal attacks cannot be simulated.

A target that "bobs" and/or "weaves" can be constructed with the expenditure of a few dollars and a couple of brain cells, and is far more representative for street-training purposes.

The competent shotgunner either "leads" a clay bird or swings "through" it as he trips the trigger. Unfortunately, on human targets it's not that easy. Because you are responsible for the projectiles you throw downrange, you have to be *dead on* with your hits—and humans don't move in as *predictable* or *smooth* a line as do clay birds.

And that is the gist of the problem.

The trick with a well-operated, weaving training target is that the trainee cannot predict its every movement—if he doesn't do *everything* right, he will not hit the desired area. And that's as much as you can ask, short of laying out big dollars for one of the prohibitively expensive (and mechanically unreliable) electronic and pneumatic systems.

Most of the time you will be extremely fortunate if the vital impact area on an attacker isn't moving up and down *and* sideways, unless he's at contact distance, in which case there's good news and bad news. The good news is that he's extremely easy to hit; the bad news is you're about to be stomped to pieces.

Okay, so how do we start working on some serious street-simulation drills?

CHAPTER 7

THE REALISTIC MOVING TARGET

Test Drill Number 1 was the quasi balloon Demi-Presidente.
Test Drill Number 2 follows.

Handgun Test Drill Number 2:

1. Set your bobbing/weaving target into *jerky, unpre-dictable, fluctuating* motion; step back 5 yards; begin firing *accurate* rounds at the X-ring, facing straight on to the target. Not too difficult, right? Right.
2. Repeat the drill, firing continuous individual rounds as quickly as possible, but maintaining accuracy. Not too difficult, right? Right.
3. Repeat the drill, this time firing two rounds each time, the second following the first as quickly as you can guarantee a good hit in the vital zone. Not too diffi-cult, right? Uh . . . maybe.
4. Repeat the drill, firing one *accurate* round to the head. Not too difficult, right? Uh . . . wrong.

Let's start over.

1. Step back 7 feet from the target and 10 feet to the right.
2. Begin firing accurate individual rounds to the near side of the X-ring—remember, we're supposed to be simulating a three-dimensional human target. Not too difficult, right? Well . . .
3. Repeat the drill, firing continuous individual rounds to the near side of the X-ring. Not too difficult, right? Well—if I could just practice for a while first . . .
4. Repeat the drill, this time firing two rounds each time to the near side of the X-ring, the second following the first as quickly as you can guarantee a good hit in the vital zone. Not too difficult, right? Uh-oh.
5. Repeat the drill, firing one accurate round to the head, bearing in mind where the hit would need to impact if the target were 3-dimensional. Not too difficult, right? Uh-oh.

We seem to have a slight problem: Our "patient," who *always* fired twice at the X-ring from 10 meters in under 2 seconds and shot 5-inch groups, took *longer* and got *worse* hits on the torso of a weaving target at *half* the distance. The head shots were extremely difficult. (Remember how he sailed through the Demi-Presidente head shots?)

As soon as the target was *angled* but still at approximately the same distance—total disaster. The bottom line? For real, unless on the same level and facing straight on to an unmoving target, firing rounds in pairs to a cadence is begging for trouble.

Fortunately our "patient" discovers this on the range and not in the street, like so many others. Or would he merely have been labeled as just one more who "panicked and didn't focus on his front sight"?

It is easy to ridicule someone who missed his mark in a street contact. But the truth of the matter is even if you are very well trained, Lady Luck plays a big part in your survival. There are no guarantees—all you can do is practice, practice, practice, and hope for the best.

As far as what you do for range practice once you have reached the "Presidente" stage of marksmanship and gun-handling competence with a handgun, it should be self-evident.

Rig up a target system that will *realistically* simulate a bobbing, weaving human target and work on variables of Test Drill Number 2. A little forethought and ingenuity will benefit you a lot more for serious fighting than staid, nonrepresentative range drills—but *don't forsake* the basic drills! When all is said and done, it still comes down to the basics: sight picture, trigger control, and follow-through.

Remember, too, that if the target does not move in an *erratic, unpredictable* path, you're wasting your time as far as realistic simulation goes. Hitting a rectangular target

A simple lateral runner-turned-charger. In "charge" mode, the trainee would have to side-step and take geometric angles of projectile insertion into contention—as well as a rapidly changing background. (The target—as set up in this mode—bobs, weaves, and oscillates.)

when you can *time* its predictable movement and/or appearance will merely help your sight picture and trigger control—it will not simulate *realism*.

CHAPTER 8

VITAL ZONE DEFINITION

You rig your "weaving" target system and get down to some serious handgun practice. And after much deliberate training, you begin to get gratifying results, with the bullets now impacting where they *should*, and not where they used to. Even though your prior training resulted in X-ring hits on a paper target, we've already discovered that "center" paper hits aren't what you always want for representative tactical shooting.

So now we're almost home, having tied in the already-accomplished qualities of marksmanship and gun-handling with the new-found mental aspects of target angles and motion. But there are still a couple of wrenches in the works, the first of which is "vital zone" definition under pressure.

We've already established that accuracy cannot be sacrificed—and of equally vital importance is the fact that the projectiles have to be delivered quickly. Obviously, if you have the time to deliver slow precision fire, you usually have the time to take the more intelligent path of removing your buns from the scene, and not getting into the gunfight in the first place.

Unfortunately, the scenario has dictated that you have been forced to defend yourself with quick, accurate shooting.

To date, although the training drills have been difficult, you've managed to overcome the Attack of the Killer Option Targets. Although your newly mastered proficiency has been largely responsible for your success, you have had a helping hand.

This "helping hand" was a target with squared-off edges and clear-cut, definitive hit zones—the positional relationship to each other subconsciously implanted in your thought processes. In other words, what you did was shoot at the desired portion of an easily defined overall outside dimension, making the vital zone easy and relatively quick to locate. Easy and quick, because once you'd visually established the outside borders of the target, you *immediately* knew where the vital hit areas were in relation to them, having trained on identically shaped targets so many times in the past.

Again, it's not that simple in the street.

A simple change of angle of headgear can change an easy head shot . . .

. . . into an eighth of a second delay for vital zone ascertainment before pressing the trigger.

Scenario: You are set upon by two attacking thugs, one wearing a tight-fitting T-shirt, the other dressed in a loosely flapping overcoat. Obviously it will be easier to hit the T-shirt man in a vital torso area than his compadre—only because of the difference in their clothing.

If you start unleashing projectiles in the general direction of the center of mass of Mr. Overcoat, you've just wasted ammunition, seven chapters of this book, and probably the only chance you had before he broke your bones. The point is his vital torso area will not be as easy to find in your mind's eye as was Mr. T-shirt's—and for sure not as easy or automatic as the clean-cut predetermined range target.

The reasons should be obvious, but let's lay them out anyway.

A. The irregular and constantly changing shape of the coat's outside dimensions

Similarly, merely shooting center of mass of a heavily garbed torso could result in a shallow bullet entry path, caused by optical misorientation of where the actual desired flesh and bone point of impact is located.

B. The shifting, changing color and shape patterns of the vital area (e.g., coat, moving back and forth across a white shirt front, tie flapping with his body motion)

C. The target size changing as he approaches—though this should work in your favor, as long as he doesn't launch himself at you in a horizontal tackle

Moral of the story? You have to *identify* the desired impact zone of the target before you can *hit* it, and you have to do this quickly because reaction time—or lack thereof—can kill you.

On "basic" range drills you already have *predetermined* knowledge of where the bullet impact needs to be. Not so for real; you may want to "look at people from a new angle" in your daily tactical awareness wanderings. Study a couple of boxing reruns, a Bogart movie or two—even a couple of cartoons—and observe how people and animals move.

If ignorant both of your enemy and of yourself, you are certain in every battle to be in peril.

—Sun Tzu, *The Art of War*

CHAPTER 9

SHOOTING ON THE MOVE

Once you've worked the target system from all angles and begun achieving consistent vital zone hits—both torso and head—it's time to move on to the second wrench in the works. This is the problem of body movement—*yours*.

It is not unrealistic to think that you may have to shoot while "on the move." In fact, many law enforcement teams are forced to do so by the tactical nature of some of their operations. But these fine people excepted, there is still the possibility of this situation being encountered by the individual—i.e., Joe Citizen attempting to *quickly* reach his car to effect an escape before the hoodlums beat on him.

As this is not a training manual (and makes no pretense to be), we won't discuss the sordid details of "how to" but instead will once again observe the problem areas.

You can shoot accurately from a stationary position, you can shoot accurately while on the move—you *cannot* shoot accurately while *running*.

Ergo, we have Joe Citizen smoothly but quickly moving his

buns toward his waiting vehicle, handgun in a "ready" or "muzzle-depressed" position. He has four thugs under observation but doesn't know which of them will start the violence—or, indeed, if any of them will escalate to the physical violence stage. He has a two-fold problem. He must keep all four under optical control—while he is moving rearward and/or laterally across their path—and then, if something does break loose, legally he is justified in dealing *only* with those in the group who are affecting his physical well-being. In other words, Mr. Citizen's task is now to shoot even more precisely than under "normal" circumstances—with an ever-changing background and having to overcome the urge to "rush" the shot, a common tendency when on the move.

The latter is obviously due to the "Let me get the shot off before my stride causes the muzzle to bypass the vital area" syndrome. Here is where the "always fire twice" syndrome is ludicrous and would be totally irresponsible.

For, when all is said and done, with all the extra effort required, Joe *must* still have vital zone hits—or at least "deep" angle-of-incidence bullet penetration, irrespective of whether the body parts struck were his first choice of "vital area." In other words, you may have to shoot for the gut, shoulder, or leg of an adversary because you have no other choice at that specific stage of the proceedings.

While this may be the time to stop moving and "stand and deliver," depending on circumstances, tactics often dictate that you *can't* stop before firing.

So it's back to the range one more time. Work the same original target angle and movement scenarios, but this time you are in motion as well. Start by shooting while on a direct frontal approach to the moving target; then try shooting while moving laterally across it; and, finally, practice shooting while moving in and out and diagonally toward and away from the "shootee."

Once you have this accomplished, with the hits where they should be if it were a three-dimensional target, you're almost there.

While the rear target offers a viable head shot in this scenario, a shootist stepping to the right would gain the benefit of an easier head shot and, in addition, would "open up" some upper torso availability as well.

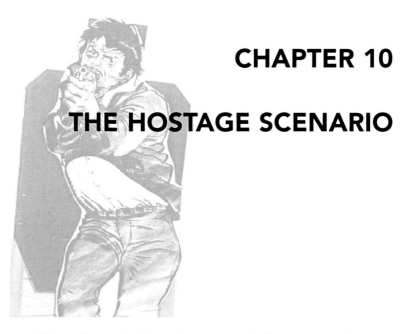

CHAPTER 10

THE HOSTAGE SCENARIO

We've all practiced it on the range—the hostage scenario. But, at the risk of sounding boringly repetitive, did we simulate *realism* during these practice sessions?

And once again the answer is—probably not.

Take, for example, the "classic" hostage-type paper target in its various forms: The bad guy usually looks like a deranged Quasimodo and is built like a family-sized gorilla. The "hostage" is invariably female, blonde, and proportioned like a Munchkin. The ogre is conveniently depicted with a full head and half torso of target area exposed, faced straight on to the trainee.

While this form of graphics gives the shooter a relatively easy target, depending on how the instructor orchestrates the drill, there is a larger and more important factor to consider: the printing of both the baddie and the hostage on a single, one-dimensional sheet of paper oversimplifies a *real* situation—and the corresponding tactical shooting required to solve the problem.

Yes, we're back to angles and movement one more time!

In essence, there is no problematical difference between this and any other paper target—all you have to do is hit a vital area on the bad guy. Sure, the idea is not to hit Blondie, but if they are both on one target plane and *cannot move in relation to each other*, it is only a slightly more difficult task than the normal one of defining the vital zone on a single target before you engage. This, *irrespective* of whether or not you have the overall target attached to your moving target system.

So what to do? Logically, the idea is to have at least two separate targets, minimally one of which is capable of being moved *erratically* and *unpredictably* in relation to the others. Even if a single bystander is stationary and only Quasimodo does the bobbing and weaving, your training goal will be achieved.

The importance, however, of the target motion's *necessity* to be *unpredictable* cannot be overemphasized. If the "baddie" moves in a smooth, pendulum-like manner, the trainee can "time" his shooting to coincide with the moment when he *knows* the target will appear from behind the "hostage."

While this is fun and promotes trigger control, again it does nothing to simulate realism, which must surely be the objective of serious defensive small-arms training.

The fore-and-aft spacing of the separate targets in relation to each other is important. This is merely an extension of the basic "angle" logic discussed in preceding chapters. Obviously the separating distance needs to be at least 8–12 inches to simulate three-dimensional torsos and heads. Once this has been done, it immediately brings up the question of the much-maligned and misunderstood shotgun.

Many defensive shotgunners are unaware of the *necessity* to pattern their gun *yard by yard* with the shot ammunition they are carrying for street use. The purpose of the exercise is to find out not only what size group your specific barrel will print a specific pellet size and brand of shot, but also to determine what the gun *will not* guarantee under various tactical circumstances. Also, it is as well to remember that there is always the chance of a "flier"

Better than nothing, but this one-piece, one-dimensional target is a "gimme" for an accomplished shooter.

More of a challenge and more beneficial for a trainee would be two three-dimensional targets moving erratically and independently of each other.

pellet every time you fire a shot cartridge.

The bottom line is that a hostage situation will undoubtedly have to be handled differently with a shotgun than it would be with a single-projectile weapon, unless there is a slug in the chamber. Apart from the ever-present possibility of a flier, the fact remains that a shot load forms a *cone* after exiting the barrel.

If you shine a flashlight at a wall 20 yards distant and then at one 5 yards distant, the projected beam is seen to be bigger but has less reflected light intensity from the 20-yard distance. Compare a shot charge to the light beam and you have pellets penetrating instead of light rays; all else is similar.

We now have a gigantic problem because of the inherent

vagaries of the shot pattern, changing distances to the target, and target angle and movement. (Incidentally, there is a general consensus that shot patterns enlarge by 1 inch for each 1-yard increase in distance from the target. Don't believe it—or, for that matter, that because your gun barrel has a certain choke constriction, it will place a certain percentage of shot into a target at a specific distance! Pattern *your* gun yard by yard—*every* shotgun barrel pattern is different than the next.) *Overall* pattern diameter is what you need to know.

We return full circle to the hostage scenario, armed with our trusty 12-gauge, a pocketful of buckshot, and patterning information pouring out of our ears. We are *ready*, pal! Or are we?

Let's take it one step at a time.

Phase 1: If both targets are stationary, all you need to do in a full-frontal situation is quick-mount the gun and hold off enough to miss the hostage but still get enough damaging pellets into the "shootee." More on the "enough" later . . .

Phase 2: We skip this step (a smooth "pendulum" target movement) because it is totally unrepresentative of human body motion, as mentioned several times previously in the text. So far so good, but here's where the trouble starts.

Phase 3: Set your bad guy target into *erratic* bobbing and weaving motion, and then observe the difficulty factor.

Phase 4: Step off to the side to get a "clearer" shot at the baddie—and you find you have to change your point of hold to "farther back" on his body or head because of the "cone" configuration of the pattern. (Remember, Blondie isn't expendable.)

Phase 5: Approach the target on the move, first frontally and then diagonally.

Clear the shotgun, sling it, and turn to Chapter 11 for an analysis of the nightmare . . .

CHAPTER 11

REALISM

The analysis brings home some horrendous truths, the first of which is the fact that you can never *guarantee* the safety of a hostage because there is *always* the potential of a flier pellet. Second, unless *both* targets are stationary and face-on, you will not be able to shoot as quickly as you can on stationary or pre-dictable, smooth-moving range targets—because for real *you don't know whether you'll be making a torso or head shot until an opening presents itself.* Hopefully, the abductor will surrender, and you won't even have to shoot. Third, you have the problem of the ever-changing pattern size going hand in hand with a change of target distance.

Let's sum up the situation: You have to deal with a crazed hophead, who's yelling and screaming and dancing a Beagle Boogie while he's got his arm—and the biggest knife you ever saw—wrapped around Blondie's torso. He's backing out of the supermarket in an attempt to escape, while you pursue with the 12-gauge.

You also have to deal with an angled, three-dimensional, errat-

A relatively simple but realistic target scenario (Blondie is the only non-moving target; camo-baseball-hat wearer is the required shootee). There is ample target availability . . .

ically moving target; ever-changing pattern size data; and the possibility of a flier—all this while shooting on the move. But you shoot anyway.

The day is saved. Blondie is unscathed, and Mister Q is down. Unfortunately, so is 4-year-old Suzy, who was hiding behind "Fruits and Vegetables" and who took two of the 00 buck pellets

Realism

. . . but shootist must continuously keep track of both the foreground and the background.

that bypassed baddie because you had to "hold off" to avoid hitting Blondie—the hold-off angle now much wider than you used on the one-dimensional, nonmoving range target. It's too complicated, you had too much to deal with, and sooner or later something had to go wrong.

If you don't have slugs, transition to a handgun. If all you have is buckshot and you don't have a clear shot—*don't shoot*!

Typical crowd scene—six targets, rear four moving; man with dark Stetson is the "bad guy."

The shotgun is a great weapon, but there are times when its limitations will hamper your ability. Most of the time in hostage situations, armed only with buckshot, it won't be as easy as they said it would be in boot camp. (And that doesn't mean an M4 carbine will be any simpler. Yes, you are now firing a one-piece projectile—but you could do that with a 12-gauge slug. Your problem now is a minimum 2-plus inch boreline/sightline differential at close quarters. And you'd better take that into consideration on a surgical shot fired at an intermittently obscured target, or Blondie is going to eat lead.)

CHAPTER 12

TARGET SYSTEMS

There is a myriad of target systems available for range training—cardboard, paper, steel, plastic, and video systems among the principle ones. What follows is an analysis of some of the products commonly used in current *defensive* small-arms training procedures—bull's-eye targets, for our purposes, will not be discussed in this text.

The first under observation is the cardboard target, usually used on the firing range to indoctrinate trainees in the basics of marksmanship and various tactical body positions. Appearing in one or two forms, it is almost invariably in option style (humanoid in shape, with a squared-off head and torso) or fashioned after the B-27 (a black humanoid silhouette printed on a rectangular background). The option cardboard target is usually buff colored or of camouflaged configuration.

If basic, frontal marksmanship is the object of the exercise—and all the tactical problems discussed in Chapters 1–11 are, for the moment, *not* being addressed—the option target is less forgiving of shooter error than the full-size B-27. But under these circumstances, any bullet holes outside an 8–10 inch "A" zone should be regarded as nonscoring, for obvious reasons.

The B-27 is scored thus: 5 points for a 10-, 9-, or 8-ring hit; 4 points for the 7-ring, and 3 points for *any* other hit touching the black. Obviously this results in many shooters scoring a 60 percent average without once hitting the 7-ring!

As the 7-ring is wider than the average-size man's entire torso (the 8-ring is wider than most humans standing side on), trainees are being recorded as 60 percent competent when they are, in fact, not even capable of inflicting a *peripheral* hit on a nonmoving, average-size human. This lulls the trainee into a false sense of security, which is not beneficial to him, to say the least. The last place he needs to find out the facts of life is in the middle of a confrontation in the street.

Since the rationale behind defensive training is to ready oneself for potential real-life encounters, range work *must* simulate street realities—and one of the areas to be considered is a realistically sized target and vital hit zone. You can't put water wings on a neophyte swimmer, place him in the shallow end of a swimming pool, and then expect him to be able to scuba-dive off the Great Barrier Reef three days later. He will drown through *no fault of his own*.

Probably the most commonly used target is the printed paper form, usually stapled to a cardboard backing on the firing range. This again usually follows the traditional option shape for range drills, while graphic "human" targets are available for more realistic simulation.

While everybody's second cousin has produced his own design on the paper option's basic outline—usually by means of a modification of a military camouflage pattern—you are still reduced to one essential: once the trainee becomes accustomed to the design graphics, the target offers no more of an identification problem with one design than it does with another.

While some designs are undoubtedly better than others, especially in the areas of graphics and vital zone placement, the underlying benefit is obtained not so much by the design as *how* you utilize the target on the range.

The common misconception is that the target will *always* present more of a marksmanship problem at a distance than it will close up. Not so *for real*, as evidenced by the Quasimodo-Blondie debacle.

Sure, on a training range, if the shooter has the *same* target at 3 yards as he does at 25 yards, the 3-yard situation is easier to handle. But that's where the fallacy of the training comes into play. On the street, a 3-yard tactical situation could very well be much more difficult to handle than a 25-yard scenario, because *the target is not the same as on the range*—and neither are the arc of fire and the tactical considerations.

So what do you do to get a running start for reality? *You modify the target on a regular basis.*

Merely extending distance to the same old target, day after day, lulls you into a rut—you do have to concentrate more on sight picture and trigger control, but all the while the implanted thought in your mind becomes, "Close up I *must* shoot fast; far away I can afford to slow down."

Well, you dumped little Suzy because you tried to rush a close shot—so that didn't work. Obviously, on occasion, you can't afford to take all day either, but training to get a balance between speed and accuracy can better be improved by constantly modifying the range target as opposed to merely practicing on the same target at longer distances. Certainly it makes the range training more complex, but how serious are you about improving your fighting ability?

How do you "modify" the target? Fold over the edges of the target, blocking out *portions* of the torso and head X-rings; this also results in irregularly shaped perimeter borders. The objective now is to impact the target *only* in the remaining portions of the X-rings that are still visible. It is not enough just to avoid hitting Blondie—in this case, the folded-over sections—you still must have hits *only* in the vital zones. Anywhere else and either you have an ineffectual hit or Suzy has bought it again.

So it's back to the drawing board. Start with very basic range drills, using your modified target. Each time you change the target, fold the fresh one differently and staple the targets at different angles and heights on the cardboard backing.

Once you're satisfied with the basics, mount a folded target on your "weaving" system and practice as many variable scenarios as you can think of.

Second to last, try the Demi-Presidente, with one of the targets attached to your "weaver."

Soul destroying, isn't it? The sad fact is this puts you where your training regimen should be—10,000 miles from boot camp and 10 yards from reality.

Finances are always a consideration in these days of fast-rising costs. If your purse strings are strangling you, there is a quick and inexpensive way to make your own "option" targets, shown below. The brainchild of Las Vegas resident Joe Williams, the tar-

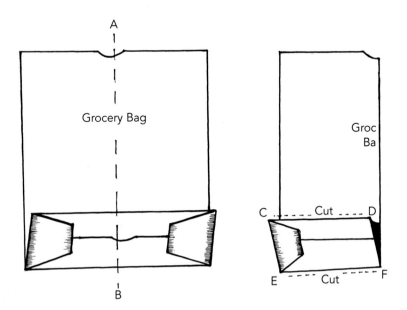

get consists of simple components: brown paper grocery bags and a pair of scissors. Each bag supplies two targets, and the "operation" runs thus:

One longitudinal north/south cut splits the grocery bag into two halves. An east-west cut along each of the folded creases that formed the bottom of the bag when it was whole completes the job. Unfold the half on which you've just completed the double cut and bingo—an "option" target (see diagram on previous page).

Another two slits on the other half and you have a second target. Quick, inexpensive, and ideal for your purposes. If you have to get more exotic at this stage, a few quick spurts from an aerosol paint can supply a camouflage design.

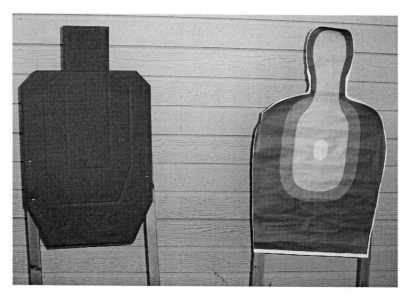

Standard option target pictured alongside one designed by the Royal Canadian Mounted Police. These targets are ideal for logging numerical qualification scores but not optically representative of a moving human assailant.

CHAPTER 13

TARGETS—
GRAPHIC AND STEEL

More expensive but also more realistic than the standardized range target is the graphic paper target. Several companies manufacture these, and (as with everything else) some are better than others. Probably the ones that possess the most attributes are those made in Belgium under copyright license to Police Judiciaire de Liege or those produced by Law Enforcement Targets, Inc.

These preferred targets come in two sizes for distance simulation in subdued natural colors. The targets are of both genders, are multiracial, and have both good guy and bad guy depictions. Overlays are also available to alter the "threat" status of the target. The only downfall of these—and, for that matter, any other graphic target—is the fact that they are one-dimensional.

While the Belgian targets do depict varying body positions, their scoring areas are perhaps a little generous. Once again, when used for street simulation training, angled hits must be taken into consideration.

Several other companies offer graphic targets with a shooter always facing straight on to the trainee, with a handgun invariably

A small selection of one-dimensional paper targets manufactured by Police Judiciaire de Liege, Belgium, and Law Enforcement Targets, Inc. Often used in live-fire "shoot houses," they offer some form of full-frontal realism for a trainee but can result in misleading marksmanship diagnosis if fired upon from an acute angle.

depicted in a classic isosceles position in front of the target's chest area.

In reality, the bigger the perceived threat, the more likely the trainee's tendency to succumb to tunnel vision. Often, under these circumstances, people shoot at what triggers the stress—in this case, the *large* bore of a *large* gun—instead of concentrating on the target's vital zones. In the case of this graphic target, the shooter gets good hits by pure dumb luck because his mental trigger (the target's pistol) *happened* to be depicted in front of the target chest area. Beware!

Possibly the only targets that currently circumvent the three-dimensional problem are the few plastic molded units. They are, however, expensive and don't last past one arduous multi-trainee training session.

Target life is about 1,000 rounds before the chest cavity and head will need to be replaced. The invaluable assets of such a target are obvious: longevity, realism, and the ability to have a crouching, lying, kneeling, or standing target that can be fired on from any angle. One must, however, keep track of hits, good or bad, or much of the benefit of live-fire drills will be lost in a ventilated target surface and nobody will know who hit what or where.

One of the things to evolve from the Age of Aquarius is the video target simulator. While it is expensive, the interbranching capability of the unit gives the trainee an ongoing scenario. This scenario continues in direct response to trainee marksmanship *and* tactics. Beyond the financial reach of the Common Man, it is excellent for maintaining the skills of trained agency personnel, not only from a marksmanship perspective but also to check observation and decision-making skills.

And last, but not least, we come to the reactive steel target, in its many shapes and forms.

Since the inception of John Pepper's "Poppers," steel targets have become all the rage. Steel, in its various configurations, is probably the most widely used and abused target material in operation today. Like everything else in defensive training, it is easy to incorrectly diagnose results and be deluded into a false sense of security.

Steel targets are, on average, psychologically easier to hit than nonreacting paper or cardboard for two reasons:

A. You have instant gratification of the resultant sound if you impact it anywhere.

B. You have instant gratification seeing the target fall if it is of the "keel-over" reactive type—if you hit it almost anywhere.

Note the word "anywhere" in A and B.

Here's where the incorrect diagnosis creeps in. If you avoid the overbearing tendency to focus your vision on the target and do it "right" (i.e., focus on the front sight and use correct trigger control), you will hit the target somewhere, and it reacts.

Take the Pepper Popper, as an abstract example. It is

humanoid in shape and hinged at its base. You set it up on the range and calibrate the target so it will fall over only with a well-centered torso hit. Hits any lower on the target will not have enough impetus to push over the target because of its low fulcrum. Step back to a safe distance and fire one round. Over goes the target. You go home, elated with your prowess. Another trainee appears on the range, steps over to lift up the target for reuse—and wonders who the idiot was who left a fresh bullet splash 1/8 of an inch inboard of the top of the target's skull.

The point is *check where the bullet impacted*, after firing. Steel targets, for the most part, are very forgiving of relatively poor hits simply because they often "react" to a poor hit. This is often the case on Pepper Poppers, when trainees who are accustomed to firing torso hits in pairs hear two "pings" as the target falls—and walk away content. Unfortunately the target is often riddled from knees to skull—poor marksmanship at best—but the target is hardly ever checked for points of impact once it has fallen over.

Another factor to beware of with reacting humanoid steel targets is the tactically angled shot. First, because most of the time the target is shot face-on to avoid ricochet problems (denying tactics), and, second (and conversely), if you do have enough arc of fire to cover the ricochet, the target may not fall to a correctly placed angled shot because of the calibration (which has to be set for frontal hits).

The moral of the target story?

- Ensure that you make an *honest* appraisal of the drill you have just completed, including checking the impact points on the target.
- Make the required hit zone of a realistic size for the selected drill you wish to practice because, most times on steel, a hit "anywhere" is mistakenly regarded as a good hit.

If it weren't so time-consuming, it would be more beneficial to practice on small balloons fluctuating in the breeze . . .

The final potential hitch comes with the use of reactive steel for the shotgun "hostage" scenarios. It is a common practice, but bear in mind the earlier supermarket scenario. You cannot afford to hit the hostage, but you *must* get enough pellets into the baddie's *vitals*—and you are responsible for the terminal resting place of *all* pellets, including those that bypass the target.

Let's face it: even if you miss the hostage, *peripheral* hits on the baddie won't solve the problem for real, and it doesn't help the situation any by hurling half a dozen pellets of a nine-pellet load down a crowded supermarket aisle, either.

You have to be more critical of your shotgun training than any other weapon because of the geometric limitations of shot patterns. A *peripherally hit* steel target that falls over doesn't usually represent a *solidly struck* human.

For true benefit you have to be brutally honest with yourself on the training range.

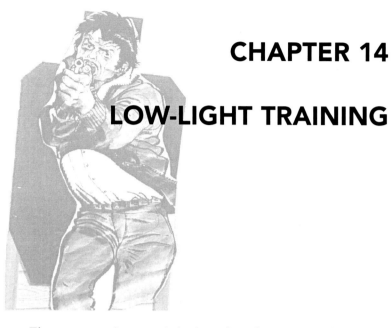

CHAPTER 14

LOW-LIGHT TRAINING

The sun goes down and shadows lengthen. Soon it is twilight, then night. Visibility deteriorates—and, all too often, so does the logic behind the trainee's instruction. For example, what is the point of practicing reloads like crazy during daylight training hours and then totally ignoring the subject during night training exercises?

The stock answer for a handgun is to tuck the flashlight under your arm and proceed with your "normal" reload. Wonderful, except unless you want the flashlight to fall on the floor, you have to remember to put it under your strong-side arm for a semiauto pistol reload, under your weak-side arm if you use the common weak-hand reload for a revolver, under your strong-side arm for a strong-hand revolver reload . . .

Isn't it getting a teensy-weensy bit complicated? Does the KISS principle ring a bell?

Try jamming the flashlight under *either* arm in a kneeling, sitting, or prone position—and *guaranteed* it will fall during a reload. Or did you practice from the standing position only, ignoring

Now you see him . . .   . . . now you don't.

kneeling, etc., merely because the sun had set?

Again, this is not a how-to instruction manual, so techniques aren't being discussed. The point is that the reload can be performed smoothly and quickly with the flashlight retained in your weak hand, ready for *instant* use immediately after the reload is accomplished. And the bottom line is your reload technique is *simple and sure*, day or night.

These matters need to be addressed during range training, not when the feces is busy impacting the oscillator.

So now you have it all worked out—and it goes down for real in the street. Fortunately, you are armed with your trusty pump shotgun. Unfortunately, you realize you're doomed again. The friend who forgot to mention the flashlight reload technique also forgot to mention that just because you change weapons

Without night-vision equipment or a high-intensity flashlight, such as one of these produced by Surefire, you cannot fight effectively in dim-light conditions.

doesn't mean that you can fire "blind"—learn the flashlight shooting/reloading techniques for all the weapons you use for self-defense!

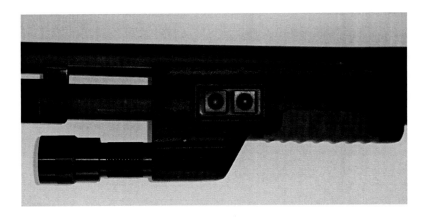

The author prefers dedicated light attachments for shoulder-fired weapons, such as this Surefire unit mounted on a Remington 870.

Granted, there are several good attachments available that allow the flashlight to be mounted to the gun—but you'd better have a back-up flashlight technique at your fingertips. Murphy's law affects only the Good Guys.

Obviously for teams, permanently affixed flashlights are the way to go, especially for shoulder-fired weapons, which are predominantly the team-operator's primary weapon. This text is, however, primarily for the lone operator's edification but might dictate similar equipment. Whenever possible, use the right tool for the right job.

While the general consensus of opinion is "if it's too dark to identify your target, it's too dark to shoot without the aid of the flashlight," the truth of the matter—going on actual documentation—is that the majority of cases report "dim-light" shootings as opposed to "black." Under these murky circumstances, tritium inserts in metal small-arms sights could make the difference between precision hits and peripheral hits.

If you can't see your sights, you can get close but you can't *guarantee* the hit. If the target is identifiable but it's too dark to "pick up" your sights, tritium is the answer. Be warned, however, that the sights can be seen in the dark from *above* and behind the shooter out to a distance of about 40 feet.

And last—but absolutely not least—learn and practice every flashlight technique you can. Whatever you can execute in ample ambient light you *have* to be able to achieve in dim-light circumstances, or you're just kidding yourself on your potential ability.

Just as everybody practices pistol tactical reloads on the range but speed-loads in battle, the average trainee doesn't put in nearly enough proportionate dim-light training hours relative to that which he expends during daylight.

CHAPTER 15

ONE-HANDED MANIPULATION

Pull off two of a flea's legs and command it to jump. It jumps.
Pull off another two legs and command it to jump. It jumps.
Pull off the last two legs and command it to jump. It doesn't jump.
What does this prove? Pull off all a flea's legs, and it becomes deaf.

Draw your pistol and fire six rounds strong-handed only; reload using both hands; then transfer the gun to your weak hand and fire another six rounds weak-handed only.

Sound familiar? Sure it does—it's your regular generic "qualification" drill.

What does it prove? It proves that you will be shot in your strong-side arm after firing six rounds and completing a reload.

Try this on for size:

Draw your semiauto pistol with your weak-side hand, fix the malfunction you caused by limp-wristing the gun after the first shot—*weak-handed only*—and then fire a head shot on your weaving target *weak-handed only*.

Ludicrous? Getting into the esoteric?

Think about it.

The primary assumption is that you will receive an injury after the fight starts. Many has been the time people have taken a hit before they could clear leather. Ergo, learn to draw the handgun weak-handed; you may have to do it for real.

Several of the semiauto pistols will malfunction when fired one-handed because of poor technique, weak shooter stature, or mechanical idiosyncrasies. Whatever the root cause, you are sitting with a malfunction—and only one usable arm. Learn to fix it on the range, not in the street. (Don't forget you need a system that will work for either hand in standing, kneeling, or other positions.)

The head shot too difficult? Tell that one to the monster who's just shot you in the arm and is moving in for the kill. Intentionally going the easy route on the training range is merely making it potentially more difficult for the street.

Better yet, *carry a minimum of two guns*.

As with the flashlight techniques and reloads—or anything else, for that matter—learn left and right one-handed operation of *all* your defensive weapons.

The unwritten rule for all but immediately clearable malfunctions is naturally to transition to a backup gun—if you have one. Whatever system you choose, *have a plan*. For example, under certain circumstances you may elect to transition to a handgun because you feel a weak-handed shotgun malfunction clearance is just too much to handle in that situation. But ensure that you have the ability to execute all your mechanical maneuvers *before you hit the street*.

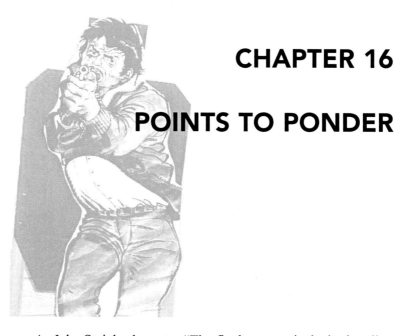

CHAPTER 16

POINTS TO PONDER

As John Steinbeck wrote: "The final weapon is the brain; all else is supplemental."

The gun is merely the means to an end—useless without thought processes guiding it. Practicing on staid, unrepresentative terrain and targets gives a false impression of how potentially difficult street shooting can be.

This is the basic premise of this book. Simulating reality—as best you can—on the training range is the *only* way you can even begin to attain skills necessary for self-defense. The trick is to sort the chaff from the wheat—the representative from the unrealistic.

Targets have been discussed from many perspectives in the text to date, but there are several other subjects worth considering. The following are some points to ponder.

Most training ranges are flat as a pancake and marked off with various distance-to-target lines (e.g., 5 yards, 10 yards, 25 yards). First, this gives the shooter a smooth, stable platform to shoot from, which may not necessarily be the case in the street. If you have the availability, practice on uneven terrain and when it's raining, cold, etc. Again, it's a matter of becoming used to all conditions—weather, terrain, difficult target scenarios, etc. The more difficult and realistic you make the range situation, the easier a street situation will be for you to handle, bearing in mind that *safety is primary* during training—all else is secondary.

The second downside of a "normal" training range—distance line markers—invariably leads to the trainee forming mental images of the target size at *specific distances*. Because the same target is invariably used day after day, and because the trainee has been orchestrated into *always* firing "X" amount of rounds at this target from "X" distance in "X" amount of seconds, he becomes a mechanical robot on the range—Pavlov's pooch.

Comes down to a street situation at 18 yards, and what does he do? He tosses a coin in the air and uses either his 15-yard or 25-yard "system" because he hasn't practiced at 16, 17, 18, 19, or whatever yardage. This can be disastrous, especially with a shot load. But the bottom line is that the trainee is now firing rounds into the street like a mechanical vegetable because of the shortsighted regimentation of his training. He has no accurate judgment of distance, target size, rate of fire, etc.

The objective of defensive shooting is to impact your assailant with whatever it takes to cause him to cease hostilities. Your primary concern must be *accurate* shot placement, coupled with as much speed as you can generate—but accuracy *cannot* be sacrificed.

The root cause of the majority of misplaced shots in a confrontation is speed—shooting too fast; the urge to beat him to the punch. The trick is not to swing and miss; it is to land the punch before he does.

While alacrity is essential, being eulogized as the fastest-shooting corpse in town isn't the answer. And while none of us likes dodging bullets, the only answer is to pace your fire to the tactical situation in which you've become involved—and it will be different *every time* because of motion, target size, light conditions, innocent bystanders, weaponry, etc. Sometimes it will be faster than "expected" range times, most of the time slower.

Once you start racing your motor, you will crash and burn. You're a better-trained driver than he is. You know how to take the corner at 60 mph; you know he's capable of only 55 mph. But you see him in the rearview mirror—and try for 70. So you slide out, and he comes past—at 30 mph. You tried to outrace him *and* yourself, and, as always, you lost.

The faster beyond your *guaranteed* maximum you try to shoot, the more the basics of sight picture and trigger control go by the board—and you miss your mark.

They told you on the range that you can drive at night at 60 mph. They forgot to tell you that most of the time for real all you have is parking lights. You can't speed when you don't have convenient high beams.

Accept basic range drills for what they are: good for improving or maintaining mechanical skills but still *basic*. The street is always an *advanced tactical drill*, irrespective of your mechanical ability.

You will have only one bad drill in the street . . . your last.

EPILOGUE

   As stated so often in the text, this is not a training manual. The book was written in the hope that somewhere in these pages lies at least one useful fact—but primarily it was written to promote serious thinking about defensive small-arms training. The text is not a criticism of current training systems or drills—it is merely an overview of points to ponder. Photographs are for illustrative purposes only and were not "snapped" on a shooting range, as can clearly be seen by the ballistically unsafe background.
Additionally, for safety reasons, deactivated weapons were used, even when utilizing a remote camera.
   Maybe the bad guy is faster or more accurate, or has plain dumb luck. There's nothing you can do about that.
   But it would be nice, just once, for the Good Guys to have the edge.

ABOUT THE AUTHOR

Louis Awerbuck is a director of Yavapai Firearms Academy, Ltd., a mobile training school devoted to the improvement of small-arms training and tactics. He was formerly Chief Rangemaster at the American Pistol Institute under Col. Jeff Cooper, as well as a former adjunct instructor for the Central Training Academy, Department of Energy. He is the author of the monthly "Training and Tactics" column for *S.W.A.T.* magazine, of which a compilation of columns have been published by Paladin Press under the titles of *Tactical Reality* and *More Tactical Reality.* He is also the author of *The Defensive Shotgun* and has been featured in three Paladin videos, *The Combat Shotgun, Only Hits Count,* and *Safe at Home.*